J'AIME PARIS

Photographs since the Twenties

by ANDRÉ KERTÉSZ

EDITED BY NICOLAS DUCROT

GROSSMAN PUBLISHERS
A Division of The Viking Press   New York

1974

Acknowledgments

The author wishes to express his appreciation to Elizabeth Kertész
for her faith and partnership and to Nicolas Ducrot for his under-
standing and spiritual communion during the preparation of this book.

Copyright © 1974 by André Kertész
All rights reserved
First published in 1974 by Grossman Publishers
625 Madison Avenue, New York, N.Y. 10022
Published simultaneously in Canada by
The Macmillan Company of Canada Limited
SBN 670-40470-5
Library of Congress Catalogue Card Number: 74-4706
Printed in U.S.A.

DESIGNED BY ELIZABETH KERTÉSZ

I write with light
and the light of Paris
helped me express what I felt
and what I feel: *J'aime Paris.*

*J'écris avec la lumière
et la lumière de Paris
est ma bonne copine.*

A.K.

14

15

A MONSIEUR DE VOLTAIRE, PAR LES GENS DE LETTRES
SES COMPATRIOTES, ET SES CONTEMPORAINS. 1770.

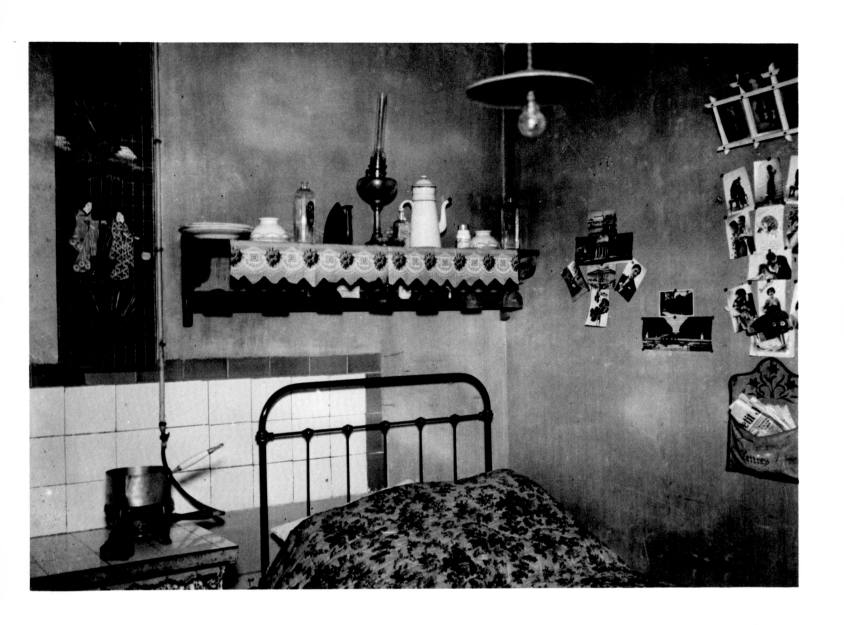

91